Redefined by Grace

Redefined by Grace

Discovering Who God Created You
to Be Despite Your Struggles

Bongi Argyrou

RESOURCE *Publications* · Eugene, Oregon

REDEFINED BY GRACE
Discovering Who God Created You to Be Despite Your Struggles

Copyright © 2025 Bongi Argyrou. All rights reserved. Except for brief quotations in critical publications or reviews, no part of this book may be reproduced in any manner without prior written permission from the publisher. Write: Permissions, Wipf and Stock Publishers, 199 W. 8th Ave., Suite 3, Eugene, OR 97401.

Resource Publications
An Imprint of Wipf and Stock Publishers
199 W. 8th Ave., Suite 3
Eugene, OR 97401

www.wipfandstock.com

PAPERBACK ISBN: 979-8-3852-4094-4
HARDCOVER ISBN: 979-8-3852-4095-1
EBOOK ISBN: 979-8-3852-4096-8

VERSION NUMBER 03/10/25

Scripture quotations marked (NIV) are taken from the Holy Bible, New International Version®, NIV®. Copyright © 1973, 1978, 1984, 2011 by Biblica, Inc.™ Used by permission of Zondervan. All rights reserved worldwide. www.zondervan.com The "NIV" and "New International Version" are trademarks registered in the United States Patent and Trademark Office by Biblica, Inc.™

Scripture quotations marked (ESV) are from The ESV® Bible (The Holy Bible, English Standard Version®), copyright © 2001 by Crossway, a publishing ministry of Good News Publishers. Used by permission. All rights reserved.

Contents

Preface | vii

Chapter One
You Are Not What They Call You | 1

Chapter Two
The Grace to Adapt and Not Die | 8

Chapter Three
Life In Abundance | 12

Chapter Four
Battle of the Mind | 20

Chapter Five
The New Beginning (Letting Go) | 27

Chapter Six
You Are More Than Your Calling | 34

Chapter Seven
What Is Your Identity? | 39

Chapter Eight
What Are Your Calling, Gifting, and Talents? | 44

CONTENTS

Chapter Nine
How To Use Gifts and Talents | 51

Chapter Ten
Who Is God (The Character of God) | 56

Chapter Eleven
What Christ Says About You | 64

Preface

FOR THE LONGEST TIME, I was introduced as Noli's daughter—the one who was killed by her husband. It was my identity: the child of a murderer. For me, this meant I always had to check my heart. In case an emotional outburst might make people think I was about to kill someone, I responded by crying when I was upset. Even though my dad was usually mild-tempered, I had made the enemy's lies my truth.

We all search for who we are instead of whose we are. Our identity is defined by our upbringing, culture, or even the country we are born into. We never stop to think about what happens when all we define ourselves by falls away. What becomes of us then, and who do we become?

Our identity should always be based on the One who made us. He says in his word, "Heaven and earth will pass away, but my words will never pass away" (Matthew 24:35 ESV). His word is true; he is the word.

—Bongi Argyrou

Chapter One

You Are Not What They Call You

Whenever well-meaning members of my family introduced me, I was Noli's daughter—the one who was killed by her husband. I was the girl whose mother was murdered by her husband, my father; I was the child of a murderer. The shame that came with that was indescribable. When introducing myself, I always omitted that part; I would just be Bongi or Pat, nothing more, nothing less.

Being the child of a murderer meant I had to hide and lie. To some, my aunt was my mum, and to others, my mum died in an accident, which technically might have been true; it was just not the whole truth. I avoided talking about my parents because it brought shame, and I thought people would pull away from me. I mean, how many of your friends' mothers were killed by their dad? Where I lived, no one else had had this experience.

Living with this reality meant that I hated being treated differently. Afraid of expressing my emotions, I wanted to be at peace with everyone and keep everyone pleased with me. If I tried to speak my mind, people would say I was cheeky like my mother. I did not want to do anything my mother did; maybe that's what got her killed.

As a young girl and teenager, I was who my parents were. I could not separate myself from their mistakes or even their good attributes. No one explained to me that I was my own person who can be judged on their own merit. We all struggle with who we are and with the turbulent sea of emotions and hormones going through us, it's hard to figure it all out.

My parents were kind, generous, and loving people, but could not stand each other at times, and all this was lived openly for their children to see. The abuse was awful; he would beat her until she no longer moved; most nights, I buried my head in my pillow to not see. To avoid hearing disturbing sounds, I learned to become a deep sleeper. Seeing the bruises in the morning was not as bad as hearing the gut-wrenching screams. This was my life, and it was "my normal" even though it never felt right.

We also had good times; like any family, we had dinner together, joked around the table, and told stories. I loved meat and still do; my dad would always leave some on his plate for me. We spent Saturdays with my dad braaiing, my mum doing laundry, and us kids playing and helping out here and there—normal family things.

I loved my dad. I would wait for him outside our house every night, run to him, and carry his bag home. He would leave a treat for me in the bag, even if it was just an apple. On Fridays, he would bring chocolates or something for the kids; he was mostly a good dad. After the incident, I didn't know how to feel about him and relate to him, which brought a lot of confusion to me.

About a month after my mum died, my uncle's wife wanted to take me to a family planning clinic; she was convinced I would fall pregnant and become more of a burden to others. I was called the lazy sister that no one wanted. My nickname was Mrs Cowen; my cousin's grandmother said I reminded her of her former boss as a domestic worker. She said I should marry rich, so I could hire people to do things for me; this was an ongoing joke about my future.

As a child, it cut deep. I felt incapable of taking care of myself. As I got older, I worked harder to prove I could take care of myself.

It's interesting how the enemy doesn't need much to disqualify us.

During the conversations of what would happen to us because my mother was gone and my dad possibly facing jail time, I think I overheard a conversation, or someone might have told me, that the family could take my siblings, but not me. Apparently, I was my mother's favorite and was spoiled.

Unfortunately, the part about being my mother's favorite didn't stick. Knowing that I was deeply loved by my mother would have given me confidence in seeking to love and be loved, but nope, the enemy made the negative stick. This lie stayed with me for most of my life: no one wanted me, and I was rejected.

Rejection found a home in my heart, and it became all I knew; I deserved nothing more. Even if someone became close to me, eventually, they would leave; I expected them to. Why would they want me? My parents did not love me enough to make it work, and my family did not have a place for me. I did not belong anywhere; this rejection affected my friendships and relationships. I became a people pleaser to ensure that no one would leave me; yet, because life happens, they eventually did, and my wounds got deeper.

The enemy kept these thoughts and feelings rotating in my mind and heart even after I started separating myself from what my dad did or the alcohol that seemed to rule our home. I couldn't get away from myself, and it was so painful to live in that turmoil; it became who I was. I identified as insecure, and I didn't know what peace felt like.

Although not excluded from society physically like a leper, emotionally I was. I internalised everything that I was called and felt I had no right to refute it. It was the truth to everyone, including me—but not to the Lord. He came close to me, just as he did with the leper that no one wanted to be nearby. "When Jesus came down from the mountainside, large crowds followed him. A man with leprosy came and knelt before him and said, "Lord, if you are willing, you can make me clean" Jesus reached out his hand and touched the man. "I am willing," he said. "Be clean!" Immediately he was cleansed of his leprosy" (Matt 8:1–3 NIV). At first, I thought it was just pity, but He proved that he loved and wanted me.

Jesus's compassion had nothing to do with feeling sorry for someone. Instead, he understood their pain and suffering and wanted to heal them of it. He does the same for you and me today. No matter what our pain looks like, he wants to bring healing to that area.

My healing began on a Friday afternoon when I asked a friend if I could go with him to church. On that Sunday, the Lord took me to the front of the church, as if to declare, "I want her." Despite this affirmation, doubt, and insecurity still plagued me. I fought Him and questioned everything, expecting Him to leave me because that is what life was for me.

I remember saying to Him, "I know you died for the entire world, but what does that look like for me? Am I just another person you had to save?" The questions reflected my insecurity, not his heart for me. I did not see myself as special to him or anyone. Salvation felt like a default. I was just another person who got roped in with the rest and gets to be called a Christian. I know now that it's not true because scripture says that no one can say that Jesus is Lord without the Holy Spirit (1 Cor 12:3) which means his Spirit works in us; then, we can confess that he is Lord. He chooses us (Eph 2:10).

The lies of the enemy don't change; he always uses the same tricks for all of us, and we believe him because we don't know any better and even when we do, we don't believe it about ourselves. Our heavenly Father is so good though, that he wrote a love letter for us. He gave us 66 books of testimonies of his work in humanity. We need to read his word and ask him to make it come alive to us so we can hear what he has to say to us and about us.

I know my story tells of a tragedy that doesn't happen to everyone, but I also know that no one has a perfect life. We have all faced some tragedy in our lives. The lies that I had made my truth were never true; whatever you have heard about yourself is also not true, because scripture says in (Eph 1:4 ESV) "even as he chose us in him before the foundation of the world, that we should be holy and blameless before him. In love"

Therefore, take the time to dispel all the lies of the enemy and let him renew your mind with his truth.

What names were you called while growing up that you began to call yourself or identify with?

_____

_____

_____

_____

_____

Scriptures

Isaiah 43:1

"But now thus says the Lord, he who created you, O Jacob, he who formed you, O Israel: 'Fear not, for I have redeemed you; I have called you by name, you are mine.'"

1 Thessalonians 5:5

"You are children of the light and children of the day. We do not belong to the night or to the darkness."

1 John 3:1

"See what great love the Father has lavished on us, that we should be called children of God! And that is what we are! The reason the world does not know us is that it did not know him."

Prayer Starter

Thank you, Lord, that you have redeemed me from the pit, and that I no longer respond to or identify with the names I have been called or even called myself. Thank you that I am your beloved child, a co-heir with Jesus Christ my saviour. Father, I ask that as you restore me, you would even change my birth name if it doesn't fit with your purpose for me. Call me what you named me before I was formed in my mother's womb. Teach me to see what you see when you look at me. Help me know who I am in you. Tell me the names you call me, like I am your beloved child, chosen and set apart. In the wonderful name of Jesus Christ, my Lord and saviour. Amen.

What name/s and/or scripture did the Lord give you in response to the prayer?

_____

_____

_____

_____

_____

Own Prayer

_____

_____

_____

_____

YOU ARE NOT WHAT THEY CALL YOU

Chapter Two

The Grace to Adapt and Not Die

THERE WAS NO ESCAPE or happy place in my life; it was my life, and I had to either adapt or die. So, I spent most of my life wishing I would die and that I had never been created.

Life felt like a never-ending punishment to me. Why would anyone choose this? To me, life meant suffering and my heart continually being ripped from my chest; just when I put it together, it happened again. Anxiety was a familiar friend. At least I knew what to expect from it. If I closed my eyes long enough, I would fall asleep, and it would stop. Death was what I looked forward to—to finally be free and hopefully be at peace.

My life was a rollercoaster of emotions that I could not control. I spent so much time crying and asking God for answers. I knew that God was real, but He could not possibly care about me or what happens on this earth. Everyone just did what they wanted or felt was right for them. I imagined that He could not wait to be done with us and often wondered why He did not start over with humanity, a world without sin and sinful humans; a do-over sounded great.

The church we attended taught that maybe one day God would let us into heaven because only He knows our hearts. So, every day you work hard to make sure that maybe one day God chooses you; all your misery will be gone, and you will live in paradise playing with lions and zebras. They don't believe in hell, so I never worried about being tortured for eternity but being completely erased from existence, which seemed like a dream to me.

When I learned about Jesus coming back, it became my daily prayer because clearly, life meant misery until He came back. There was a comfort in believing that all his children would be spared from the Lord's wrath, and I hoped I fit the criteria.

Sometimes, we miss the point of the Lord's grace and end up feeling frustrated with life because we think we have to do everything ourselves; this is what I grew up thinking. If I wanted the change, I had to work extra hard for it, otherwise, it wouldn't come. Our misconceptions of God sometimes keep us from experiencing him fully for ourselves. We blame everything on him without realizing that what happens to us breaks his heart.

The Lord doesn't do things as the world does. There are small and big victories in this life depending on the challenge we are facing. We all want a happy ending but that only comes through Christ. He is not the Father who only disciplines; he first gives love and then corrects us in love.

Eventually, I learned to adapt and started asking the Lord about my life, the reasons I was created, and what I bring to this world. I learned that God doesn't waste; he makes everyone for a purpose and cares for each person he has ever created. I don't have to fit some criteria. I just have to follow him and do what he says, and when I get it wrong, he gives me the grace to do better.

Scriptures

Exodus 34:6

The Lord passed before him and proclaimed, "The Lord, the Lord, a God merciful and gracious, slow to anger, and abounding in steadfast love and faithfulness.

Proverbs 25:2

It is the glory of God to conceal things, but the glory of kings is to search things out.

What misconceptions do you have about the Lord and the reasons he created you?

_____

_____

_____

_____

_____

How has God changed those misconceptions and shown you who he is and who he created you to be?

_____

_____

_____

_____

_____

Prayer Starter

Father God, there are so many things I have believed about you: that you don't care about us or anything that is going on in the world. We are so used to the bad in the world and the mistakes of our parents that we have come to expect it from you. Father, I repent from this way of thinking and ask for your forgiveness for not recognising the gift you have given us through the suffering, dying, and resurrection of your Son. Lord, please teach us anew about who you are. Help us to hear your voice and see you through the pages of scripture and not to be content with what we have been told or experienced but to search you out for ourselves. Thank you for the grace and love that reaches us even in our worst possible moments. In the merciful name of Jesus Christ, who died and rose for us.

Own Prayer

_____

_____

_____

_____

_____

_____

_____

_____

_____

Chapter Three

Life In Abundance

I LEARNED WHAT IT means when the word says, "Therefore, my beloved, as you have always obeyed, so now, not only as in my presence but much more in my absence, work out your salvation with fear and trembling, *for it is God who works in you, both to will and to work for his good pleasure*" (Phil 2:12–13 ESV). Yes, we have to work out our salvation, but it is from the place of love, and God is the one who enables us through his Spirit that lives inside of us; it doesn't mean that "maybe" I will go to heaven.

It means we are saved by grace as scripture says (Eph 2:8–9), but we also have to live right and not take this grace for granted (Rom 6:1–2) by doing whatever we want and living in sin. We must continue to choose a life of purity, of drawing close to the Lord, knowing his will, and loving him and others.

It is good to listen to sermons, but it is imperative to read the word and pray for revelation with the help of the Holy Spirit. We are people who live in a broken world; therefore, we make many mistakes, including misinterpreting the scripture, sometimes even to suit our circumstances or make it work for us.

Yes, it is the Holy Spirit who works in us, but God is a gentleman, and he doesn't force us. We have to come to an agreement and work with him.

God was so far from me, and my life was full of shame, rejection, and pain that made me feel like my heart was only beating because I kept taping and gluing it. So, when I became born again, it still felt like I did not belong. God was going to kick me out at any moment when he realizes I am just too broken, that I am not a virgin, I cannot be saved, and I am not worth the effort.

No one told me that when someone gets saved, even though the slate has been wiped clean, the memory is not. The insecurities are still alive and well, and the enemy does not stop attacking; he probably goes even harder because he does not want us to choose life and experience healing.

I lived with a broken heart and thought it was always going to be that way; that's just life, or so I kept telling myself. Until the Lord said to me one day, "Bongi, I can only work with what you give me; I have given you free choice." I had to make a choice to give him my everything, to not hold onto anything he didn't give me; but it's easier said than done.

As much as I heard the words and chose to give him everything, I did not understand what it meant. I thought I came to the Lord to get fixed. Did I not say the salvation prayer? After all, I am born again, so why can't it just be all right? Unfortunately, this is a misconception we have when we pray the salvation prayer. If I am born again, why does it all still hurt? Why am I still lost? How can I let the Lord work in me? Which pieces do I give him first?

I remember saying to Him, "Lord, why did Jesus Christ die for us and still let us be born, leave us here on earth to still suffer? What was the point?" Then I read (John 10:10): "The thief comes only to steal and kill and destroy; I have come that they may have life and have it to the full." So, my next question was, what does it mean to have life in full (abundance)? How can I, with all the pain I have in my heart, have it? I longed to say the words of the Psalmist: "In your presence, there is fullness of joy."

The enemy isolates us and makes us believe everyone else is happy and has it together, except for you. You did not get saved right, or Christ's salvation is not enough for your mess, which is actually pride. What Jesus did on the cross is enough to save anyone. That was the point; he did what we couldn't do for ourselves, and it is finished.

The enemy keeps us stuck and trapped in our minds. We do not talk to anyone about our struggles because they will see just how broken we are and wonder how we got in. These are some of the lies the enemy tells us to prevent us from experiencing what God has for us.

Of course, we will not know everything on this side of the grave, but we must trust God and believe that because we love him and are called according to his purpose, he is working it all together for our good (Rom 8:28).

The Lord also gave me (John 16:33): "I have told you these things, so that in me you may have peace. In this world, you will have trouble. But take heart! I have overcome the world." So, I started to understand that being born again does not mean I float away from all that is wrong with the world; I am still in it, and I still have to keep fighting. What it means is that I can overcome it because he did. I need to hold on even tighter to the Lord when it all comes crashing down. I don't live in ignorance but face up to what is going on in the world and keep praying like my life depends on it, because it does.

My constant prayer was, "Lord, how do I overcome the world and experience your freedom and abundance when all it seems to do is swallow me whole?" I lived a very defeated life; nothing seemed to take away the pain that kept me up at night and soaked my pillow. Sorrow was my friend; I smiled at everyone every day and responded with the usual, "I am good," even though this was not a reality for me.

This may sound like a one-off conversation with the Lord, but it was not. It took years of praying and trying to hear His voice, to understand that He wants to speak to me and show me His heart. My healing didn't happen overnight or as soon as I received Jesus into my heart. In fact, some days my brokenness still creeps in, and the enemy reminds me that my earthly father took a life, and I have his DNA; therefore, I'm no good. My mother drank too much to numb her pain, so why would the good God of the universe want to be with me? How am I different from them? If I start drinking, I am going to become an alcoholic like her and if I get mad, I am going to kill someone like he did; it is what I know, so why would I do any different?

In those moments, I forget about all that the Lord has done in my life, and I am back to being an unworthy orphan that the wonderful God of the Universe could not possibly be bothered with, the least on His list. Most days, I understand that Jesus died for me, to cleanse me and give me a new life; other times, I disappear into the cloud of unbelief: Jesus dying for our sins was not personal, I am not special, and I am a default.

Although this might not be your story, the enemy's tricks are the same; just because you grew up in a Christian home does not mean the enemy lets you have a perfect life, that you never respond to what people call you and the things that question who you are. It happens to all of us; the enemy of our soul is here to steal, kill, and destroy, as it says in John 10.

Life can really challenge and change our identity or rather the way we see ourselves, so we begin to describe and introduce ourselves by our sin or circumstances: the familiar "Hi my name is John, and I'm an alcoholic." You can swap it for anything you have done or been through: a liar, failure, murderer, or victim. As hard as it is, none of it is permanent; only God is.

We all carry a misconception of our identity with us; it becomes who we are and determines how we live our lives. We conform to the rules of society that divide us according to what we have or can offer financially, what we look like or the continent of our origin.

We live in an unforgiving world that marks us according to our mistakes or that of our parents. The shame follows us, and we merge with it until we become shame itself. Our life ends up belonging to the sin or mistake and no matter how much we try to rise above it, it feels like someone just keeps pushing the lid down, and the only way to escape is through death.

But God!

Life in abundance does not mean life without challenges. It is how we weather the storms and move forward after the challenge; how we keep praying even when we do not see the other side. It is laying it all down at the foot of the cross and saying, "Jesus, take my burden and my yoke; I cannot anymore." Most of all, it is realizing that he promised to never leave us nor forsake us, and he keeps all his promises. "I will never leave you nor forsake you" (Heb 13:5b ESV).

Matthew 24:13 says the one who endures to the end will be saved; this is repeated many times in the book of Revelations. We have to continue overcoming and trust that God knows best. I call this life's training ground; it will test you and what you have put your faith in; if it's not Jesus, the only one who saves, it will all crumble and leave you empty. If your faith and hope is only in Jesus, you will rise victorious as he promised.

What sins or guilt of past sins still keep you in a cage and prevent you from experiencing life in abundance?

_____

_____

_____

_____

Scriptures

Matthew 11:28–30

"Come to me, all who labour and are heavy laden, and I will give you rest. 29 Take my yoke upon you, and learn

from me, for I am gentle and lowly in heart, and you will find rest for your souls. 30 For my yoke is easy, and my burden is light."

Psalm 119:33–40

"Teach me, O LORD, the way of your statutes; and I will keep it to the end. 34 Give me understanding, that I may keep your law and observe it with my whole heart.35 Lead me in the path of your commandments, for I delight in it.36 Incline my heart to your testimonies, and not to selfish gain!37 Turn my eyes from looking at worthless things; and give me life in your ways.38 Confirm to your servant your promise, that you may be feared.39 Turn away the reproach that I dread, for your rules are good.40 Behold, I long for your precepts; in your righteousness give me life!"

Philippians 4:7

"And the peace of God, which surpasses all understanding, will guard your hearts and your minds in Christ Jesus."

Proverbs 37:5–7

"Commit your way to the LORD; trust in him and he will do this: 6 He will make your righteous reward shine like the dawn, your vindication like the noonday sun.7 Be still before the LORD and wait patiently for him; do not fret when people succeed in their ways, when they carry out their wicked schemes."

Prayer Starter

Lord Jesus, thank you that you don't call me by my sin or the mistakes I have made. Please teach me to separate sin from who I am and how to walk in your way, to open my heart to your love, to let it heal and restore me, to fill me with life in abundance and to experience your peace that surpasses understanding. Thank you that you can break any cage, even the ones I have built for myself. Gracious Father, I submit my brokenness and trade it for your wholeness and joy. Please help me to continue to submit with every step I take, with every season and phase of my life. Thank you that you give us beauty for ashes and that nothing is impossible with you, no matter how far gone we may think we are. It's never too far from your saving hand. Thank you that Jesus died and rose again so that I can have a full life. Lord, hide your word in my heart so that I may not sin against you; teach me how to walk rightly before you. In Jesus's life-giving name. Amen.

What scripture/s did the Lord give you as your freedom promise and meditation verses?

_____

_____

_____

_____

_____

Own Prayer

_____

_____

_____

_____

_____

_____

Chapter Four

Battle of the Mind

Suicidal thoughts plagued me most of my teen life and well into my twenties; thoughts would take over my mind, and I would just fall apart. At age seventeen, I tried once. I read up on pill overdose and thought that was my way out. To my surprise, I woke up the following morning; nothing had happened. I still cannot explain it. Maybe I did it wrong, or maybe the Lord spared my life. I have thought about that day often and wondered why I did not die.

Once, I mentioned to my younger brother that I would like to be next to die; I received an unexpected answer: "What about the pain you will be causing the ones you leave behind?" I didn't have an answer for him; in my pain, I had never thought of their pain, or how finding me dead in my bed would affect them. He must have been fourteen when we had that conversation; I doubt he remembers it, but for me, it was my first wake-up call.

The look on his face told me he also did not want to live through another loss. In a way, it pulled me out of my own head and made me realize I was not the only one hurting or broken; my siblings would be devastated by another death, and I couldn't do that to them. Unfortunately, for most people who commit suicide, their own pain is so overwhelming that they cannot see other people's pain. Like me, they just want it to stop or to not feel anymore.

After I was married, I would think of my husband and the kids whenever the thoughts would come. One year, none of that mattered. The thoughts in my head were so overwhelming, and I just did not see my family or empathise with their possible pain. This time, a casual remark by a friend that there is no repentance on the other side of the grave made me think twice. Therefore, one cannot commit suicide. The strange thing is I had never told her about my thoughts, and I don't even remember what we were talking about. I wanted to leave this world, but not being sure of what would happen on the other side of the grave, I could not carry it through. The sudden fear of being lost was strange, since I had never wanted to exist to begin with.

It was comforting to know that the Lord always sends someone to say something we need to hear, even if they do not realize the significance of the conversation.

The enemy does all he can to destroy us and when he cannot, he keeps us busy on who we are not, trying to take away our identity; we must fight and choose to believe the truth every day and focus our minds on what God says. The good news is, we don't have to do it alone; we overcome by the blood of the lamb and the word of our testimony (Rev 12:11 ESV). I am so grateful we have the finished work of the cross and the indwelling of the Holy Spirit, which makes resisting the enemy so much easier. Jesus fights for us and alongside us as we keep declaring our dependence on him.

God often fights on our behalf in battles we don't even see. There are battles we must fight, like those in our minds. During my many prayers to the Lord about dying, He said to me, "If you die without victory over this, then death is your saviour, not me; I want you to fight!" From that day on, I made a decision that death would not be my saviour but Jesus alone. Thoughts still come sometimes because the enemy always tries to push the spots he has succeeded in before, but now I fight with every weapon at my disposal: prayer, tongues, worship, praise, and the full armour of God.

I no longer just roll over and let the enemy have his way. I am not in agreement with the devil; I'm in agreement with my saviour, Jesus. The enemy hates me; he hates you just as much. He will not rest until we are destroyed, but the Lord promises victory. Pray for endurance; we are on the winning side!

At a prophetic training, one of my fellow mentors told me God wanted to give me the hammer of the Lord to break the altar like they did in the Old Testament. I had been battling the whole week with bad dreams and felt like I was in a fight. After the class, I was so mad! I said, "Devil you are a coward! Go fight someone your own size, who can see you." That night, I had an attack. It interrupted a dream I was having. I saw a window open and felt the spirit of fear and anxiety overwhelm me.

I woke up and declared out loud, "No! I do not accept your attack, in Jesus's name! The Lord rebuke you, satan!" It still lingered, so I kept praying. I went to lay hands on my kids and prayed over our home and my husband. I have had a similar experience before after praying over someone and felt attacked by the spirit of anxiety that was on them, but this one was different. If I let it, I would lose my mind. I could see myself in a corner rocking back and forth, completely trapped.

Over the next few days, I was aware of the Holy Spirit rising up to fight for me, even though the anxiety spirit lingered. I had to keep resisting it and let the Holy Spirit fill me with peace. I was reminded of (Deut 30:19 ESV): "I call heaven and earth to witness against you today, that I have set before you life and death, blessing and curse. Therefore, choose life, that you and your offspring may live,"

We have to choose life every day, sometimes even moment by moment. There are no in–between or grey areas in life; with every choice we make, we are either choosing Jesus or the devil. We forget this so often and end up letting the enemy win because we think it's a little white lie.

I know that you might be facing the biggest battle of your life yet during this season, and you are not sure what to do. Draw close to the Lord, and he will draw close to you. This is not a one-off moment; it's a continuous moment-by-moment decision. Choose him and choose life. The season will pass, and you will find him faithful as he cannot deny himself (2 Tim 2:13).

Life can be overwhelming, and the enemy doesn't stop attacking. Whether or not you have had a similar experience or find yourself contemplating suicide and the feelings of defeat seem like it is all you are ever going to feel, remember that it is not true! The enemy is lying to you. Jesus loves you and completely wants to heal you. Call on him and lay it all at his feet, even if it is being angry with him; he can take it all. In fact, he has already taken and done it all for you. You are dearly loved, even though you cannot sense it, by our Lord and Saviour, by those around you, and by your community in Christ (if you do not have one yet, pray for Jesus to help you find one close to you). Maybe like me, those around you are also focusing on their own pain and not seeing yours. Seek help and open your heart and mind to someone.

In 2 Cor 10:5, it says, "We destroy arguments and every lofty opinion raised against the knowledge of God, and take every thought captive to obey Christ." This should be our daily practice as believers in Christ.

What thoughts hold you hostage that you need to dispel today?

_____

_____

_____

_____

_____

Honestly tell the Lord what you are feeling and going through. Lay all your burdens at his feet.

_____

_____

_____

_____

_____

Scriptures

John 16:33 NIV

"I have told you these things, so that in me you may have peace. In this world you will have trouble. But take heart! I have overcome the world."

Matthew 28:18 NIV

"Then Jesus came to them and said, "All authority in heaven and on earth has been given to me."

Romans 12:2 NIV

"Do not conform to the pattern of this world but be transformed by the renewing of your mind. Then you will be able to test and approve what God's will is—his good, pleasing, and perfect will."

1 Corinthians 2:16 ESV

"For who has understood the mind of the Lord so as to instruct him?" But we have the mind of Christ."

Galatians 5:22 NIV

"But the fruit of the Spirit is love, joy, peace, forbearance, kindness, goodness, faithfulness."

Prayer Starter

Father, in the name of Jesus, we submit our minds and our thought patterns to you. Please renew our minds as you promise in your word and give us the mind of Christ. Lord, we do not want death to be our saviour but Jesus alone, who already died for us and paid for all our sins, pain, and failures. So, from this moment on, we lay down our burdens at the foot of the cross and pick up your grace, joy, peace, love, endurance, goodness, kindness, faithfulness, gentleness, and self-control. Thank you that all your gifts are free and without repentance. Lord, we receive your plans, vision, and dreams for our lives and submit what we thought might be or should be to you. We are your children made in love and for love, in your image; we are a new creation in you, in the powerful name of Jesus Christ, Amen.

What words of encouragement or scriptures did the Lord bring to mind to comfort you in tough times?

_____

_____

_____

_____

Own Prayer

_____

_____

_____

REDEFINED BY GRACE

_____

_____

_____

_____

_____

_____

_____

Chapter Five

The New Beginning (Letting Go)

"The fear of the Lord is the beginning of wisdom, and knowledge of the Holy One is understanding" (Proverbs 9:10 NIV). I believe this fear means holy reverence, acknowledging that he is God and that he is in control; making him Lord over our lives helps us have access to wisdom, knowledge, and understanding. This means we don't only say it with our mouths but reflect it in our actions; we know we are accountable to him.

Yes, there's grace for everything we get wrong or for making mistakes, but that doesn't mean we disrespect our Lord. Grace is for when we miss it, not when we deliberately live in sin. Paul asked "What shall we say then? Are we to continue in sin that grace may abound? By no means! How can we who died to sin still live in it?" (Rom 6:1–2). We must get to know our creator, give him the position he deserves in our lives, and live according to his guidelines.

Just a simple example. Once, I was trying to decide on where to publish my book. The prospective book deal on offer looked so good that I thought the Lord couldn't possibly say no; after all, I was doing it for him. My husband reminded me that disobedience doesn't have to be something big as we might think. It is also the little things we do, like stepping outside his timing and taking a deal that looks like it's from him but is not. I prayed more about it and the Lord said no; therefore, I had to turn it down.

It was really hard typing that email; I had to submit to his "no," even though I didn't understand it. The fear of the Lord makes me want to do whatever he asks of me without having the full picture. Even if the fear of him not opening another door creeps in, I have to fear him more and submit that fear to him. He is Lord over my life and decisions; those that don't have his "yes" should make me uncomfortable. I wait for his "yes"; no matter how long it takes, I don't move without it.

We are not a church trend or people followers but Christ followers. We are his church and body; therefore, our lives are not our own (Jer 10:23 NIV).

So, how do we let go, forgive, and begin again without asking the one who started it all? It says in (John 1:1–4 ESV), "In the beginning was the Word, and the Word was with God, and the Word was God. He was in the beginning with God. All things were made through him, and without him was not anything made that was made. In him was life, and the life was the light of men. The light shines in the darkness, and the darkness has not overcome it."

The world speaks of re-inventing yourself, that everything is in your control; you just have to "will" it in. But what happens when we fail again, and it all crumbles? We did not make ourselves; therefore, we can't save ourselves. God made us; we look to him to lead us.

God created us in love. We are not experiments gone wrong. So, who else can we ask about starting over or how to do it and for the grace to do it? Everything that was made was made through him. We belong to him and no one else has the ability to create us or recreate us; we are a new creation in Christ because he knows the blueprint of creation. Even though we are made in his image, we still cannot make people. Only he chooses the image of himself he wants to portray in each of us.

What does it mean to begin letting go and to have freedom in Christ in a world full of labels and chains? How do we even begin to turn our lives around and find out who we are? It all begins with a simple prayer:

Lord Jesus, come into my life and become Lord over my life. I believe you are the Son of God, you died for my sins, for my spiritual, physical and emotional healing, to give me a new life and access to a relationship with You, the Father and the Holy Spirit. Lord, come and renew my mind, help me to see myself through your eyes and understand my position in your Kingdom. May your will, purpose, and life reign over me forever. In the most powerful name of Jesus, Amen.

Note that it begins with this prayer, which means it is the beginning of a journey. Receiving Jesus into your life is not a magic wand that makes everything that is wrong and painful turn into dust, and you're suddenly lifted into glory. It is a process of constant surrender. You have to consciously let the Lord in over every corner of your heart and let Him stitch every broken piece, and man, is it a painful process! But it is so worth it. Sometimes He brings in memories you had buried so deep that you had forgotten they existed.

The reason He brings it up is that we feel pain we do not even understand, or we are unable to pinpoint the origin. When others do something or something happens in our lives, we react from a hurt we had never dealt with because we have scars on scars that run deeper than the Congo River, some self–inflicted and some by others. What I love about God is that He is such a gentle, kind, and loving Father that He does not force you or does the healing all at once. There have been times when I said, "I cannot anymore! It is all too much!" Then, He stops before nudging me toward His healing again.

Choosing healing over pain can be more painful for a while because we re-experience the pain, like rubbing salt into wounds. Salt actually helps accelerate the healing but at first, it doesn't feel like healing. Often, people give up on the process, but it is so worth it to think about something that happened to you without breaking down. You might wonder why the Lord does not just heal it without bringing it up. Well, for me, mostly it is because I need to see His hand in the pain, Him loving me in other people's choices that have broken me, and Him loving me through my bad choices.

The other side of it is that the enemy knows what I have been through and done, and he doesn't hold back when he wants to hurt me and bring feelings of worthlessness. I might bury the past, but it still happened, and he stands accusing me. As scripture says in (Rev 12:10), "And I heard a loud voice saying in heaven, Now is come salvation, and strength, and the kingdom of our God, and the power of his Christ: for the accuser of our brethren is cast down, which accused them before our God day and night."

Our healing needs to be complete, and the Lord makes sure of it. That is why He works with us to bring healing. It is an important part of us, receiving new life and living life in abundance. Does that mean trouble will be done with you? Unfortunately, not; when Adam and Eve sinned, it broke down everything in our world. We live with the ramifications of sin. Scripture says in Rom 8:19, "For the creation waits in eager expectation for the children of God to be revealed." Our healing and restoration are connected to the earth.

The earth is not breaking down because of global warming. It is the same sin that tears us apart and keeps us fighting each other that is breaking our world down; we do not need new environmental laws—we need Jesus.

The world is in pain and that includes nature; it all needs renewal and restoration. There is so much more to Christianity than dying and going to heaven. There is life on this earth; otherwise, just after Jesus died, the world would have ended, and God would have started over as he said in Revelations. This does not mean that Christianity explains everything; only God can do that. We also do not have to know everything; we just need to know Jesus and his heart for us, to trust him and to believe that he is working and waiting for the right time.

Absolutely everything we need is in God. "You make known to me the path of life; in your presence, there is fullness of joy; at your right hand are pleasures forevermore" (Ps 16:11). We must keep connecting to the Holy Spirit to get it. Why doesn't God just give it to us, you ask? Because we have to choose Him and choose life over and over until this body dies or Jesus comes back.

It's called a walk with the Lord because it never stops; it's a marathon, not a sprint, and it is meant to be enjoyed even when there is chaos in the world because He promises to give us peace that transcends all understanding. "And the peace of God, which transcends all understanding, will guard your hearts and your minds in Christ Jesus" (Phil 4:7).

God does not define us by what we have done or gone through but by His original design for us: His image. "So, God created mankind in his own image, in the image of God he created them; male and female he created them" (Gen 1:27 ESV). This tells me that even when I do not know who I am, God does because He put His image in me; he made me. Jesus died to restore God's image in us that has been marred by sin. He decided long ago who I am going to be. My gifts and talents are not only mine because I receive Christ. That's why we have many successful people who are not in Christ. "For God's gifts and his call are irrevocable" (Rom 11:29 NIV). The gifts and talents come into alignment with His purpose and plan, and they are made pure when I let him in and make him be Lord over my life.

Forgiveness is not always easy; some wounds cut deeper than others, but we know it is possible because God forgave us. He says as far as the east is from the west, that's how far he removes our transgressions from us (Ps 103:12). We also can ask him to help us let go; we don't have to do it on our own strength. He promises to help us in our weakness. Bring it in front of the Lord repeatedly if you have to until it's all gone.

Another important step in the process of growth is joining a church and committing to meeting with other believers, to encourage and help each other grow (Heb. 10:24–26). We need those who have walked with the Lord longer to come alongside us and disciple us in order for us to grow. I'm not saying our salvation should depend on other believers, but it helps to have people who understand and are on the other side of your current struggles.

Reading the Bible and praying is also important in our transformation of letting go, forgiving, and becoming healthier Christ followers who mature and are fully devoted to him.

Bring before the Lord everyone you need to forgive and ask him to help you to forgive them for whatever they have done, and to forgive yourself as well for all that you have done.

_____

_____

_____

_____

_____

Scriptures

Psalm 15:10 KJV

"Create in me a clean heart, O God; and renew a right spirit within me."

Matthew 6:14 NIV

"For if you forgive other people when they sin against you, your heavenly Father will also forgive you."

Prayer Starter

Father God, you are Lord almighty. We enthrone you in our lives and receive Jesus as our Lord and saviour. Lord, we ask for forgiveness for all that we have done to others and to ourselves; please teach us to forgive others as you have forgiven us. We ask for a clean slate, and we want to start afresh with you. Lord, take our broken pieces and mend them in your grace; make us whole in you. Teach us how to move forward from difficult seasons and not

THE NEW BEGINNING (LETTING GO)

let them trap us, even if we must start over many times in order to let go. In the healing name of Jesus, Amen.

Ask the Lord what your new beginning looks like:

_____

_____

_____

_____

_____

Own Prayer

Chapter Six

You Are More Than Your Calling

THE PAIN I EXPERIENCED pain in my life made it hard to believe that I am chosen and born for such a time as this, or that I am part of a royal priesthood. The first time I heard from a prophetic class that God was proud of me, I wept uncontrollably because I could not understand why; no one had ever been proud of me. Then hearing that God wants me to write, sing and do so much else was so overwhelming that I stopped listening because I was crying so much. Thankfully, the prophetic words were recorded; otherwise, I would have remembered nothing from that night. I listened to that recording over and over, sometimes pausing because I could not hear anymore.

My fellow class members were seeing me through the Lord's eyes, His original design for me in this life. They did not see or speak out my fears and pain or mistakes; they saw God's heart for me, which in turn made their hearts bigger for me. One cannot prophecy over someone without feeling the love of Christ for them. Something inside of you changes; the person is no longer a stranger that you were just praying for to give hope. The powerful love of Christ for this person overwhelms you to the extent that they become a part of you. I love prophecy; God is always so willing to speak words of love and healing to His people, to reveal identity in us. Hearing what God thought of me made me want to go deeper, not only to hear from others but for myself. From that moment on, I was no longer dead inside; I came alive with purpose, part of God's beautiful design.

I was not put on this earth to suffer, then die to disappear and never be remembered, or just the daughter of a murderer or an alcoholic; that was something that happened, not who I am. I am a daughter of the creator of life. He is not my earthly father, and even though my earthly father was made in the image of God, he was not God, and he made many mistakes, as we all do. The Lord's DNA in me matters more than my dad's because His blood flows through my veins. He made my parents and knew their lives and mine and He still chose to make me even through the chaos, the abuse and pain because He knew me and wanted me. He wanted me to know that I matter, and that I can make an impact in the world. I don't have to right my parent's wrongs, but I can help others to not make the same mistakes and help bring healing to those who have lived through their own mistakes and what they suffered because of the mistakes of others.

My end is better that my beginning, even if only one person experiences Christ and receives his love because I told them about my brokenness and my identity being changed from a murderer's daughter to that of one chosen, made into a beautiful fragrance, a beautiful pearl, creative like my Father. I am his and his alone.

He calls us forgiven, beloved, righteous in His word and gives us words that are personal to us because He wants us to know we are so much more than what we have been called, what has been done to us, or what we have done to ourselves.

God wants you more than anything you can ever do for him. Our ultimate purpose is to love him; that's what we are guaranteed to have through eternity. Everything else is a bonus. For me, it was amazing to hear that God has called me to teach, minister, bring healing and more, but we can get so caught up in what God has called us to do that we forget the one who has called us. We get so caught up in doing things for him and advancing his Kingdom that we forget to spend time with him.

We feel special knowing we were meant to impact the world in a unique way, and that we are not just a number on earth, but that we matter in God's plan to save the world. We can spend so much time helping others or teaching about Christ that we forget about things that seem insignificant, like playing soccer with our kids and cooking dinner for our family. Family is important to God and so it should be to us.

Being a wife, a mom, a sister, a daughter, and a friend is also an important part of my calling. I do not have to always be making altar calls or leading people in worship to feel the presence of the Lord. Sometimes, it is in speaking to my kids, making a meal they will enjoy or picking up their dirty socks.

If one looks at the state of the world, it is easy to be consumed by the need the world has for Jesus that we forget that Jesus is and will always be the one who saves, not us. Everything we do should flow from our relationship with the Lord. One of my favorite prayers is, "Lord, please help me to not work out of emptiness but from your fullness and your place of love." Writing, teaching, leading worship, and mentoring in the prophetic are important, but I am first to be a child of God, to be in a relationship with him. Do not get me wrong; God wants us to fulfil the great commission. Look at the disciples: when Jesus sent them out, they came back to him, and he would take them to a place of rest.

God would still love me even if I never did anything for him, but because I love him and he has given everything to me, I want to do everything for him. I give him my all to use as he sees fit. The other side of it is that I want others to experience his love and grace as I have, and for them to live in his freedom and one day meet him and live in permanent peace. I still have to keep reminding myself, no one is saved in the name of Sibongile Mchunu Argyrou (Bongi) but in the name of Jesus Christ of Nazareth.

What is the Lord calling you to do in this season of your life?

_____

_____

_____

_____

_____

Scriptures

Ephesians 2:8–9 NIV

"*⁸ For it is by grace you have been saved, through faith— and this is not from yourselves, it is the gift of God—⁹ not by works, so that no one can boast."*

Matthew 10:31 NIV

"So don't be afraid; you are worth more than many sparrows."

Prayer Starter

Dear Lord of all, thank you for the purpose you have placed in our lives. Thank you that you didn't create us to just live and die, but to change and impact the world around us, whether it is in raising our children, preaching the Gospel, or being kind to a neighbour and showing the love of Christ. We know Lord that all these things are a gift from you, our loving Father. Lord, we submit ourselves, our callings, and purpose to you. We ask that you order our steps, give us the vision for your plans and help us to be good stewards of your resources. Lord, we are because you first were, and we can do nothing apart from you. We want to move, live and have our being in you. Lord, be at the centre of all that you have called us to do. Teach us how to lead from a place of love, overflowing with your kindness, mercy, and goodness, in Jesus's name, Amen.

Own Prayer

Chapter Seven

What Is Your Identity?

GOD USES SO MANY things in scripture to show us our identity and who he created us to be; the fact that he created us to be his, his beloved sons and daughters remains constant.

We were made in his image, scripture says; therefore, we cannot know who we are until we take the time to understand who God is. Everything in us he put there; he knew us before the foundations of the earth, and he knitted every fibre of our being with his hands in his wisdom.

So, how does knowing whose and who you are change your perspective in life? Often, we are in need of something we are not sure of, but knowing who and whose we are helps us to understand that we were not made by chance. God didn't say "Oops! There goes another one. How in the world am I going to manage these people?"

He makes no mistakes; he has created each one of us with a purpose and for a purpose. As human beings, we crave significance because we are significant to the one who created us.

In a world that doesn't believe in God or thinks he is irrelevant today, like an old wives' tale, now more than ever it's of utmost importance to find out for ourselves what our identity is and what the thoughts of God are towards us. He says they are more than the sea sand (Ps 139:17–18).

The most important aspect of life is to be a child of God. That is our identity; we are his children. If you have children, you know how big a role you have in their lives, and the kind of responsibility you have.

I remember the first time I held each of my kids. With each of them came a part of me I didn't know existed. With my first son, I wanted to protect him, even from me. I didn't know much about parenting and had read all I could and prayed, but you never know what kind of parent you are until you actually do it. I didn't want him to be my trial-and-error child, to leave scars that he would carry for the rest of his life but to be everything God had created him to be.

I want to protect my children, provide for them, lead them well, give them comfort when they feel hurt or disappointed, correct them when they are wrong, and discipline them so they know right from wrong. The list is so long; can you imagine how our Father in heaven feels about us?

He says he saw our unformed substance (Ps 139:16), and he chose us in love before the foundations of the earth (Ephesians 1:4), so nothing else explains who we are more than being the beloved of our Lord, the King. He loved us so much that from when we fell, he already was ready to die for us because he knew that we could only be redeemed by his blood (Gen 3:15).

Nothing we do can change that he created us out of love and wants us to be with him. So many scriptures tell us that God wants to dwell with his people; almost all the prophets prophesied him being our light, and that we won't have need for the sun and moon.

He showed us an example of this when he led the children of Israel from Egypt to the promised land as a pillar of cloud by day and pillar of fire by night (Exod 13:22). He loves us so much that he wants to be with us always.

If you are still not convinced, remember that he sent his Spirit to indwell us. The Holy Spirit knows our hearts and minds and that of God our creator, and he lives inside of us. One of the greatest things I learned in having children is that God loves my children more than I love them. That is big, because I really love them; it also means he loves me just as much.

To know in your mind that you are God's child and knowing in your heart that you are his child are two different things. Head knowledge means you are cognisant of it; heart knowledge changes how you see yourself, and how you behave and treat others.

Being a child of the most powerful King and Creator, the author and finisher of life itself is a lot cooler than having Superman as your dad (he is also just a creation). He formed the universe and everything in it and he chooses to be our Abba Father; that is our identity that no one can change or ever take away, not our calling, gifts, talents, who our parents are/were, how much money we have, or where we live.

Scriptures

Psalm 139:13 NIV

"For you created my inmost being; you knit me together in my mother's womb."

1 John 3:1 ESV

"See what kind of love the Father has given to us, that we should be called children of God; and so we are. The reason why the world does not know us is that it did not know him."

Acts 17:26–28 NIV

"From one man he made all the nations, that they should inhabit the whole earth; and he marked out their appointed times in history and the boundaries of their lands. God did this so that they would seek him and perhaps reach out for him and find him, though he is not far from any one of us. 'For in him we live and move and have our being.' As some of your own poets have said, 'We are his offspring.'"

What things in your life do you see as your identity?

_____

_____

_____

_____

Prayer Starter

Our Father, who art in heaven, hallowed be your name. Thank you for being a great Father; thank you that I am your child and thank you for the privilege of knowing you as my Father. Thank you that nothing can ever separate me from your love; thank you for drawing me closer to you every day; thank you that you want a relationship with me, you look forward to spending time with me, and that you love me. Lord, I pray for anyone praying this prayer who doesn't know you as a Father, who can't even imagine you caring about what is in their hearts, that they will experience you in a new way, and that they would see you rightly, Lord. Open their hearts, Father, heal any hurt that is keeping them from experiencing you as their Father who loves them and wants what's best for them, a Father who withholds no good thing from them, and a Father who wants to spend eternity with them. Thank you that our identity cannot be taken away from us; we are your beloved children. Thank you for sending Jesus to die for us and make it possible for us to have a relationship with you and thank you for sending the Holy Spirit to live in us, for making it easier for us to feel your heartbeat and hear your voice, in the redeeming name of Jesus, Amen and amen.

WHAT IS YOUR IDENTITY?

Ask the Lord to show you how much he loves you, with a scripture, prophetic word, poem, a dream or in whatever way he wants to communicate with you:

___

___

___

___

___

Own Prayer

___

___

___

___

___

___

___

___

___

Chapter Eight

What Are Your Calling, Gifting, and Talents?

God called David "a man after His own heart" (1 Sam 13:14 ESV). "But now your kingdom shall not continue. The Lord has sought out a man after his own heart, and the Lord has commanded him to be prince over his people..." Does that mean David was perfect or did everything perfectly? Not at all. God chose David, the youngest among his brothers, from the field while he was shepherding his father's sheep.

David led the sheep exceptionally well and defended them against predators, putting his life in harm's way. When God called him, he was in the field doing the task given to him by his father. Samuel had seen all the brothers and even then, they were not sure if they should call him, so Samuel had to ask for him. David was in training to later lead God's flock; God equipped him right where he was.

We are all born with our own set of gifts and talents which become our calling; just like David, God trains us using daily activities. If someone is a therapist, God uses their desire to help people feel heard and help them arrive at an understanding or solution and draw them to him in order to grow his Kingdom.

As a little girl, I loved singing and dancing. I was the entertainer in our family and watching people smile and laugh was my favorite thing. I did not know then what I know now: I love helping people feel good and bringing them joy. I still love making people laugh and feel good about themselves; the best way for people to have consistent joy and feel love is by knowing what God says about them and how God sees them.

My involvement in the prophetic and worship ministry allows me to share the heart of God with people to help them feel comforted and loved; in turn, it blesses me to know that I have helped someone begin to realize that God loves them, that he has plans for them and solutions for the things they face.

Worship ministry allows me to enter the presence of the Lord and to usher people in. During worship, I pray for the Lord to help people experience his love. Whatever the Lord pours into me, I pour out to his people; he keeps pouring in because he is the cup that never runs dry. Sometimes, the wonder of who he makes me want to explode and other times I feel undone as the Holy Spirit takes control.

The presence of God changes everyone and everything. I have always liked journaling, but my journals were always so sad because I have always felt robbed of childhood and love. The first time the Lord told me through a prophet who has a powerful international prophetic school that I would author books and curriculums, I was shocked because, at this point, I had only written prayers, songs, and thank you notes to the Lord.

That night, I drove home in silence, thinking about where to start. Finally, I said aloud, "Lord, if you want me to write, please tell me what to write about." The first book was about purity; then I just kept going, writing about what he is teaching me. It confirmed that he has given me a ministry of grace and reconciliation. God does not only want to reconcile people to himself but to themselves and to each other (John 17). He is still giving me revelation in his own timing.

You might be thinking that my calling and gifting sound easy; I can assure you, it has not been an easy road. There have been moments of wondering why I am here, not wanting my gifts and talents because they looked unusable or because I did not know where to overflow. I still doubted that the living God could call me and want to work with me, not just to heal me but to bring healing to his people through my ministry.

My hardest work is not in activating my gifts and talents; it is in believing that God gave them to me to use. It is fighting the voice that says I am not good enough and my gifts are not good enough; the voice that says if only I sounded like that person or wrote like that, my vocabulary was not enough, and I do not know scripture well enough to write about it.

One of the incidents that affirmed me in my calling was when writing "Christ's Image in Us"; as I wrote, scripture would flow. The Holy Spirit would bring it up like without effort from me. I was absolutely flabbergasted at the work the Lord can do through me. I could never do this without him, and I am so grateful for all he is teaching me.

I went through a season of hating the sound of my voice. I couldn't stand hearing it on a recording. The Lord has been so kind to me in redeeming my sound and how I hear it. My former boss asked me to make a recording for our office's answering machine; everyone who called after hours from anywhere in the world would hear my voice. The Lord will show you glimpses of what he has for you, piece by piece to build you up, because he cares about you deeply. I could relate so many stories of how he redeemed my love for worship, from prophetic words to people telling me that my voice gives them comfort. My favorite was when singing, "I'm no longer a slave." During the first line, "you unravel me with a melody," the Holy Spirit wrapped his arms around me; it was so strong and tangible. His love and continued affirmation confirmed my calling.

Writing this, I can barely see the screen remembering the many precious moments with him; it humbles me and brings so much significance to our relationship. If he can do it for me, he can do it for you. I have done nothing special to deserve this kind of love; it speaks more about who he is than about me.

All my life, I have been told I'm not "it": not pretty enough, not smart enough, or not talented enough; everywhere I looked, there was someone better. I thank God for my sister who always told me that I was able; she always believed in me and supported me.

I have learned that God appreciates my gift and loves me using it, but most of all, He did not give me a lesser gift. I do not need to envy others or wish I could "sing better." Of course, every gift needs to grow and mature with time. I continue to work on my gifts because he promises to multiply whatever I use to serve him and share with others.

You too already know what your calling, gifts, and talents are; you just might be insecure about using them because the enemy has told you they are not good enough or you are not good enough or you just do not know where to use them. The best thing I ever did was take it back to God and seek outside help from people who care about me, asking for help, prayers, and direction. Prophetic schools are the best place to hear what God wants to say to you if you are not used to hearing and knowing God's voice, but most importantly to teach you to hear what God wants to say to you. God wants to speak to us.

Reading the Bible is also important to learn to hear and understand the voice of God. He never speaks out of character or contradicts the Bible. Get to know him in his word to know how he speaks. That does not mean putting him in a box; it just means getting to know him personally.

God wants to work with you in all that you do. You will find that like David, he is training you where you are right now. You just need to ask, "Lord, what are you teaching me, and where are you taking me?" David faithfully herded and defended his father's sheep, and eventually he did the same with God's people. That is why he was God's favorite; he was not perfect but in all he did, he did it as unto the Lord. He was also quick to repent when he sinned. In every Psalm where he felt God was not there or answering, he ended with "I know you will because you are faithful."

What is God calling you to do in this season?

_____

_____

_____

_____

_____

What is God training you for?

_____

_____

_____

_____

Scriptures

John 16:13 ESV

"When the Spirit of truth comes, he will guide you into all the truth, for he will not speak on his own authority, but whatever he hears he will speak, and he will declare to you the things that are to come."

Isaiah 41:10 NKJV

"Fear not, for I am with you; Be not dismayed, for I am your God. I will strengthen you, Yes, I will help you, I will uphold you with My righteous right hand."

Prayer Starter

Father God, we know that you have deposited many gifts and talents inside of us that we can use in ministry and outside of ministry because where we are is a place where you want us to glorify you. Thank you for gifting us with everything that we need and will ever need; thank you for continuing to multiply the work of our hands among our family and friends and in our workspace, schools, and ministries. Lord, we ask that you reveal to us your heart in the things we are already doing and show us where you are taking us next. Show us, Lord, where our gifts and talents lie, where we are already using them, and where we can further use them. Father, I pray for every heart that is discouraged and feels you are not answering their prayers or you couldn't possibly desire to work through them, be it because of sin or just lies of the enemy. I ask that you bring people alongside them who will speak your truth to them, who will point them to your compassionate heart for them. I also ask you to give them the grace of confirmation, so that they can know that you have called them by name and that you have great plans for their lives. I pray for wisdom, knowledge and understanding in all that they are doing and will do for your glory. We pray against the fear of man and ask that you will secure them in their identity and position in your Kingdom. In the wonderful name of Jesus Christ, Amen.

What is your calling?

_____

_____

_____

_____

_____

Own Prayer

Chapter Nine

How to Use Gifts and Talents

THE BEST PLACE TO use your gifts and talents is where you are. Sometimes, God calls us to our homes before he calls us to the nation or even nations. When I worked full-time in a corporate environment, I wasn't even aware of how my gifts were used until a colleague said, "You know, we were talking about you, and it's so amazing that no one walks away from you feeling bad about themselves; you say things that boost our confidence."

I did not purposefully decide to make them feel that way, but because God had gifted me with mercy and edification, it just came out without me being aware that he was speaking through me. I have also chosen to not speak negative things over people. You too can choose to build or break. No, I do not always get this right. On becoming a Christ follower, I learnt to understand my gifts through discipleship and prophecy.

It is true that there are false prophets; it says so in the Bible, but we should not throw the baby away with the bathwater. Prophecy must resonate with you; test the word given to you as scripture says in (1 Thess 5:20–21). Even though God might say something new through a prophet, most times, he tells you something you already know. The prophetic word just puts it in perspective.

God would never have told me to be an astronaut or anything to do with science. I would not even know where to begin. That is not to limit what God can do in our lives; I know he can turn stones into worshipers so he can make me an astronaut. He will always prepare us; he doesn't throw us in the deep end, and if he does, it's because he is teaching us how to get through it.

Your calling is also connected to who you are. It does not define you; only God does, but it is something that comes without you thinking about it at first. Most people think they do not know what to do but that is because something happened that made them think they cannot. I have always wanted to sing and write songs that uplift people but because my parents never saw it as a career, they discouraged me from an early age; it is a hobby not a career, and there's drugs and sex.

So, I looked for something else. At first, I wanted to be a lawyer. During my first year studying law, my dad was so proud; he introduced me to his friends as a future lawyer who would fight the injustices of the world. It made me so happy to have made him proud; it was the first time I had heard him say that. After he passed away, I started thinking that maybe this was not for me. Learning about it wase enjoyable, but I could not see myself doing it all my life. There was also no money to continue, so I dropped out.

It was never my dream; it was his, but that left me displaced. I still could not study music, so I tried other things, but nothing seemed to fit. I tell this story because like me, you may already know what you are called to do: your passions are your calling. No one is devoid of passion; if that is what people say about themselves, there is a story there; life happened, or someone changed their mind.

Start small, right where you are. For some, it might not look practical and you may not even see it. Write down the plan, as it says in Hab 2:2 (ESV): "And the LORD answered me: "Write the vision; make it plain on tablets, so he may run who reads it." This is not a "vision board"; it is God's plan that he will help you execute by his Spirit.

Ask the Lord questions about the things he puts in your heart. How do you know it is from him? He will not tell you to go hurt someone; whatever it will be, it will help people and make the lives of others better. Unless your country is at war, he will not give you war strategies, but he will give you strategies for spiritual warfare because our enemy is unseen.

In the hands of God, we are so much more than what we think, and he can do so much more, not because he wants us to just be working for him but because we are co-laborers with him (1 Cor 3:9). It is rewarding when you do something you love and see it positively affect others.

So, go out there and make a difference in all the spaces you have been called to by his Spirit.

What lies have you believed about your gifts and talents?

_____

_____

_____

_____

_____

Scriptures

Jeremiah 1:4–5 NIV

"4 The word of the LORD came to me, saying,5 "Before I formed you in the womb, I knew you before you were born; I set you apart; I appointed you as a prophet to the nations."

Ephesians 2:10 NIV

"For we are God's handiwork, created in Christ Jesus to do good works, which God prepared in advance for us to do."

Prayer Starter

Father God, I pray for every person who is not sure where to start; Holy Spirit, I ask that you minister to them; help them to see what you see and feel what you feel. I break every word of discouragement spoken to them or over them, and I cancel all the work and words of the enemy, in Jesus's name. Stir up desires inside and rekindle dreams inside of them and show them that with you it is never too late to start over and find what you have called them to do. Lord, I also ask that you show them their track record, the things they have said or done for others without realizing what they were building or what you were training them for. Open their eyes to what has been deposited into them and give them a vision for the path and work you want them to do. Thank you, Lord, that we can do all things through Christ who strengthens us. Thank you that even when it looks overwhelming to us, it is not too much for you. Lord we long to hear the words, "Well done good and faithful servant" when we stand in your presence one day. In Jesus's name, amen and amen.

Where and how is the Lord calling you to use your gifts and talents?

_____

_____

_____

_____

_____

Own Prayer

Chapter Ten

Who Is God (The Character of God)

A̲l̲t̲h̲o̲u̲g̲h̲ ̲w̲e̲ ̲c̲a̲n̲ ̲n̲e̲v̲e̲r̲ fully explain God, at least, not on this side of the grave or maybe even ever, God has revealed parts of himself that are relevant for us. Throughout the Bible, he has been many things to many people, depending on what was needed at the time.

We endeavour to explore the many characteristics of God that he has shown us through his word and our own experiences. For us to understand who we are and what our identity is, we need to first know and understand who he is.

God is our Father; unfortunately, most of us struggle with this image of God. We impose our own expectations and earthly experiences on him. When Jesus describes God the Father and their relationship, it reveals the truth of who He is.

He speaks of a Father none of us have experienced; their relationship is tender yet firm. Jesus obeys the Father out of love. Jesus said "I do that which I see my Father do" (John 5:19–20), and "if you have seen me, you have seen the Father for I and the Father are one" (John 14:7–9).

We know God the Creator because we know he made us and everything that is seen and unseen (Gen 1). We know God can make things out of nothing, and that in his wisdom he thought out the heavens and the earth and all that is in them.

God also works through his creation to create new things. Even though some people don't acknowledge him, he still creates things through them in the fields of technology, governments, or even in having children. God is the creator of it all (John 1:1-3 NIV): "In the beginning was the Word, and the Word was with God, and the Word was God. He was with God in the beginning. Through him all things were made; without him nothing was made that has been made. In him was life, and that life was the light of all mankind."

We also know God as one who is in control of nature and brings the entire earth on its knees as he did in the days of Noah. We see him as the God who keeps his promises and commands blessing on the earth and rebuilds everything (Gen 7-10).

We see Jesus calm the storm (Matt 8:35-41NIV), walk on water (Matt 14:22-33 NIV), and curse a tree to die (Mark 11:12-25 NIV). Throughout scripture, God demonstrates his power through nature. In Egypt he brought the plagues, to call the Israelites out and saves them from Pharoah.

So, we know he is powerful and has authority in all the earth and no one can stand against him. Sure, he humours the magicians from time to time but ultimately, he stands above all, and there is no God beside him. "This is what the LORD says— Israel's King and Redeemer, the LORD Almighty: I am the first and I am the last; apart from me there is no God. Who then is like me? Let him proclaim it. Let him declare and lay out before me what has happened since I established my ancient people, and what is yet to come—yes, let them foretell what will come. Do not tremble, do not be afraid. Did I not proclaim this and foretell it long ago? You are my witnesses. Is there any God besides me? No, there is no other Rock; I know not one" (Isaiah 44: 6-8 NIV).

We know God as a redeemer and saviour. Soon after the fall, God promised that Jesus would come to bruise the serpent's' head (Gen 3:15), and throughout the Bible we see how God fights for his people and, in the most amazing victory yet, Jesus died on the cross for us.

When Moses met with God in the burning bush, he asked, "Whom shall I say sent me?" God had already walked with the Israelites, Jacob's children; he had already revealed himself to be the God of Abraham, Isaac and Jacob (Israel), which means Moses knew God and the Israelites knew him as well; both Jacob and Joseph prophesied of the Exodus. God chooses to reveal himself as *I am*, the God of your Fathers (Gen 3). So, why would Moses ask who was sending him? Because many characteristics in the Bible describe God, and he needed to know by which strength or name he was being sent forth.

Moses grew up in Egypt and was raised in Pharoah's household; he knew and understood how powerful Pharoah was. He also knew his brothers and sisters would not believe him if he just said, "Come, let's go!" He had already tried to defend them once; it put his life in danger and he had to flee, so Moses was asking for God's might, the *Great I Am*, because he knew it would not be possible in his own strength.

I have always found it interesting that God called himself the God of Abraham, Isaac and Jacob. He is the God of all generations but he also reveals different parts of himself to each one of these generations under one covenant and promise.

Who was God to Abraham, Isaac and Jacob?

When God called Abram out of his people, he gave him a promise. We have already seen how God kept his promises with Noah during the flood, but the Lord's promise to Abram is about building him and making nations out of him before he even had offspring

One of the most important things to note is that God keeps his promises, no matter how long it takes. This includes even the promise about Abram's descendants being sojourners in a nation that will mistreat them.

God proves himself as the God who does the impossible or what man thinks is impossible. He sets aside one man and blesses him with a relationship with himself, land, possessions, an heir and nations added to him as his inheritance.

When Abram and Sarai go ahead of God to bring themselves an offspring through their servant Hagar, God extends the promise of multiplying Hagar's offspring to make Ishmael a nation as well (Gen 17:18–21 NIV): "And Abraham said to God, 'If only Ishmael might live under your blessing!' 19 Then God said, 'Yes, but your wife Sarah will bear you a son, and you will call him Isaac. I will establish my covenant with him as an everlasting covenant for his descendants after him. And as for Ishmael, I have heard you: I will surely bless him; I will make him fruitful and will greatly increase his numbers. He will be the father of twelve rulers, and I will make him into a great nation.'"

God is so gracious that even in our mistakes, he keeps his word, redeems every situation and works it for good for those who are called according to his purpose (Rom 8:28).

I love the generational call to serve God. Although I don't have my mother to learn from, but I pray and dream of a time when my daughter and granddaughter would learn from my faith and wisdom, that they would see the grace of God in my life and believe for themselves and their families, and that they would see God's faithfulness in my life and remember they are part of the same covenant and promise.

We see God appearing to Isaac and to Jacob with the same promise of nations and fruitfulness, but we also see him appeal to their individuality, to their unique circumstances, in different phases but from the same place of covenant keeping.

God meets us where we are. He does not say well, you have messed up too many times; I cannot forgive you anymore. His grace for us says "Come back! I love you!" We see this grace when Solomon prays that God would always hear the cry of the Israelites, or anyone who prays to him (1 Kings 8) and God grants Solomon his prayer for he is a compassionate God (1 Kings 9). This does not mean we have to abuse him and keep walking however we want, but it is where our love and fear of him come in. It compels us to do his will and live in obedience to him.

We know he is God and that he is in charge, and that he made us in his image (not the other way around); therefore, we are to conform to him, not him to us. Abraham, Isaac, and Jacob were not chosen because they were perfect or somehow escaped the effects of a sinful world.

They were chosen because God first loved them (1 John 4), before they knew about him, and it is the same for us today; he understands that we will miss it and fail but he also knows that we have a choice to keep choosing him, so we do not miss it as often.

I think God is an optimist. He looks at us and says, "Go on! I know you can resist the devil, and you can choose right" because he knows we are so much more than our sins.

The most important truth God repeats throughout the Bible is that we must follow him and no one else, and that he is faithful to fulfil his promises just as he did with Abraham, Isaac, and Jacob. We are part of his promise to them, and we are living in the promises he made to them.

Who is God to us today?

God has not changed; he is the same yesterday, today and forever (Mal 3:6; Heb 13:8). He is still kind, loving, compassionate, and full of grace. He continues to call us to himself; he still saves and more now that Jesus Christ has come to cover and forgive all our transgressions and died for all.

He is still the God who appeared to Gideon and spoke through the prophets, who calls out destiny and who meets us with relentless love in whatever circumstance we find ourselves. All we must do is to come in agreement with him and choose life (Deut 30:19 ESV): "I call heaven and earth to witness against you today, that I have set before you life and death, blessing and curse. Therefore, choose life, that you and your offspring may live."

WHO IS GOD (THE CHARACTER OF GOD)

If you have not experienced God as a Father, ask him to reveal himself as a Father to you:

_____
_____
_____
_____
_____

Which attributes of God grab your attention the most?

_____
_____
_____
_____

Write down those scriptures as a reminder of who he is:

_____
_____
_____
_____
_____

God has been many things throughout the scriptures in different people's lives. Who is he revealing himself to be in this season of your life?

_____

_____

_____

_____

_____

Prayer Starter

Father God, we are so grateful for your word that is living and sharper than any two-edged sword. We know that you have chosen to reveal yourself to us and teach us about your ways. Lord, we ask that you teach us how to dig deeper for ourselves and get to know you and your word. Holy Spirit, please give us the understanding of the Father, reveal the Father to us and his heart. Tell us the secrets that are hidden in the Bible for us to find. Help us to know you, the Father, Holy Spirit and Jesus individually and as one on a personal level. Thank you for your unfailing grace and compassion for when we miss you or what you are doing in our lives. We want to be committed students of the Holy Spirit, in your gracious and powerful name of Jesus. Amen and amen.

Own Prayer

_____

_____

_____

WHO IS GOD (THE CHARACTER OF GOD)

Chapter Eleven

What Christ Says About You

Isaiah 54:10 NIV '... "Though the mountains be shaken, and the hills be removed, yet my unfailing love for you will not be shaken nor my covenant of peace be removed," says the Lord, who has compassion on you.'

The one thing we should pray to understand and let sink in is how much God loves us, and that his love for us does not waver and will never be removed. He speaks this truth so many times in scripture, yet it is the hardest thing to receive. When we do, most of the time it's head knowledge.

I have struggled with this unshakable truth; He loves me and no matter what changes around me or what sins I have committed, he still loves me, and nothing can change that. God is pure and hates sin and what it does to us; he doesn't hate us.

If nothing else in life sinks in or takes root in your life, pray that him loving you does. It doesn't have to make sense; it just needs to be the undeniable truth of your life. You are the beloved of the Lord Jesus Christ, and he has chosen you.

When things don't go my way, and nothing seems to be working, or when I have prayed all the prayers and prayed in tongues and still don't see the Lord moving, this is what I read: "But now thus says the LORD, he who created you, O Jacob, he who formed you, O Israel: "Fear not, for I have redeemed you; I have called you by name, you are mine" (Isa 43:1 ESV). This verse is a reminder that he made me and calls me by name; I am never forgotten.

My name means gratitude (Sibongile: we thank you). I love it so much because it reminds me that the Lord is thankful for me, no matter what my circumstances look like. No matter what I have done, he is thankful for me and does not regret making me. Not everyone may think their name means something beautiful, but you can change it. Many people legally or even socially have changed their names to what the Lord calls them.

A name is important; people speak it over you every time they say it, so if your name has a negative or destructive meaning, that is what is spoken over you and everything you do. God changed Jacob's name to Israel and Saul's name to Paul because their names didn't fit God's narrative or what he has called out of them.

Every name in the Bible has meaning, even if it was just to speak of the times or confirm God's promise.

In a world full of labels and everyone choosing their pronouns, we should find out what God says about us and ask for help to see what he sees in us, and what he has placed in us. "When the angel of the LORD appeared to Gideon, he said, "The LORD is with you, mighty warrior" (Judges 6:12 NIV). Gideon was not a mighty warrior at that time, at least not in the physical. God always calls out what he has created in us: his image and our identity, not our current circumstances or fears.

Psalm 139 is one of my favorite Psalms, specifically verse 14: " . . . I am fearfully and wonderfully made . . . ." When God made us, he wasn't confused about who he was making. He didn't say let's see what comes out, or let it surprise me. He knew exactly how you would look and what you would sound like; the hairs on your head are numbered (Luke 12:7). He calls you beautiful, lovely, made in his wonderful image.

People are confused, and in seeking to find out who they are, they check with the world and follow current trends to help them develop an identity instead of asking God. It really breaks my heart to see so many children being told that it's okay to identify with a different gender or with an animal. The enemy has clouded our reasoning and sense of self so much that we see ourselves in things that don't matter, which creates more division and confusion.

God's heart is for us to know who he is; in turn, he teaches us who we are in him. A few years ago, I felt the Lord say he wanted to awaken himself in us. He told me to gather a group of women for a photoshoot. "They need to spend time with me (God)—and each hear my heart for them and know what I call them." I invited a few ladies, and the outcome was overwhelming. They all came back with beautiful words of what the Lord sees in them.

It was such a beautiful experience for me; I made a video just speaking to the heart of a woman and hearing what God wanted to say to them, especially black women who have been overlooked in every area of their lives. Please don't get me wrong, I'm not saying other women from other races don't experience displacement. I'm just speaking out of my experience of this world.

What I love about the Lord is that he sees beyond what's been said and done to us; he sees what he has created, what he has done on the cross; he sees what he has put in me and continues to build into me, and he calls me lovely, brilliant, beautiful, and he chooses me even when I don't choose him, and he would make me over and over again.

We might be growing up in a world that is imperfect and struggle to find our identity and where we fit in, but Jesus is not confused about who we are. He knows that our mistakes don't make us who we are because our identity is not based on circumstances that are constantly changing, but on him who doesn't change and will never be moved.

We are always growing and learning new things and changing our minds on certain things, but God doesn't; we need to fix our minds and hearts on him and what he calls us because even when we do something wrong, he doesn't take away our identity or his image from us; instead, he comes in with correction in love.

Genesis 32:28 (NIV): "The man said, 'From now on, your name will no longer be Jacob. You will be called Israel, because you have wrestled with God and with men, and you have won.'"

What names have you been called that you would you like to renounce?

_____
_____
_____
_____
_____

What name/s does the Lord call you:

_____
_____
_____
_____
_____

Scriptures

1 John 4:1 KJV

"Beloved, believe not every spirit, but try the spirits whether they are of God: because many false prophets are gone out into the world."

1 Peter 2:29 NIV

"But you are a chosen people, a royal priesthood, a holy nation, God's special possession, that you may declare the praises of him who called you out of darkness into his wonderful light."

Prayer Starter

Father God, thank you that you made us and that you know every single part of us; you understand us, you created us, and you call us beloved children. Thank you that you see your image in us and everything you created in us. Thank you that when we come to you, you call out what you have placed in us and draw it out. You show us how beautifully created and creative we are. Thank you that nothing you made is useless, including us. Lord, we pray that you would open our spiritual ears for us to hear what you call us, to know your heart for us as individuals and as your people. May the Holy Spirit highlight scriptures that speak of who we are in you and what you call us and create a hunger to get to know the God who made us and to know ourselves in you. Teach us not to let the world define us and make us into something we are not. Lord, whisper your sweet words to us and restore our identity in you, in the name of Jesus. Amen.

Own Prayer

www.ingramcontent.com/pod-product-compliance
Lightning Source LLC
LaVergne TN
LVHW051709080426
835511LV00017B/2806